May I Introduce You to a Friend?

Teresa Skinner   Gordon Skinner

Agnes I Numer   Ashley Flores

Onoh Kesandu Nwankwo

ISBN: 978-1-955759-24-3

Authors: Teresa Skinner, Gordon Skinner, Agnes I Numer, Ashley Flores, Onoh Kesandu Nwankwo

Illustrators: Jackson Muthoni, Julian P. Arias, Chidubem Mbamalu, "Love" Painting Larry Cole, Jackfi, Jumi Sabbagh

Order additional copies:
email: is58mti@gmail.com
www.all-nations.org
www.seldomseenpress.com

"If you don't plant something you want on your Farmland - something you don't want will grow on it.

And again, even if you plant something you want and you don't carefully tend to it, something you don't want will still grow and suffocate the things you planted.

— Faith Chidinma Metchie

* * *

We are very grateful to Mr. Larry Cole for permission to use the Love Painting. It truly tells the story.

Contents

Who is God?

We think God is created like us... He is not...

We are created like Him.

God was... Even before we were created. He has no beginning and no end. God made everything; heaven and earth and all living things. God also made man.

- God is the Creator

In the beginning, God created the Heavens and the earth in only seven days:

Day 1: God created Light and separated the Light from the Darkness.
Day 2: God created the heavens.
Day 3: God created Earth, sea, and vegetation.

Day 4: God created Sun, Moon, and Stars.
Day 5: God created Birds and Sea Animals.
Day 6: God created Land Animals and Humans.
Day 7: God rested.

When God created man, he made him out of the dust of the earth.

After God formed man, He breathed into him and man became a living, breathing creature.

This makes us special to God.

God created the Garden of Eden as a place for Adam to live and talk with Him.

- What was the Garden of Eden?

Imagine a place – the most beautiful garden or park where there is no pain, suffering or torment. Everything you need to eat grows naturally there for you.

The animals get along peacefully. No one fights or is angry; there are no bad attitudes and no unkind words. Together, God and His people walked and talked in the garden when the evenings became cool.

Everything was perfect.

This is what God made in the beginning – for the people He loved.

> And the LORD God planted a garden eastward in Eden; and there he put the man whom he had formed. 9 And out of the ground made the LORD God to grow every tree that is pleasant to the sight, and good for food; the tree of life also in the midst of the garden, and the tree of knowledge of good and evil.

— Genesis 2:8

- Where does God live?

God has His own kingdom. We cannot control Him. He is God.

God has His own culture and His own way of expressing Himself.

God lives in heaven and He can live in our hearts... If we let Him.

It is important that we know who God is and that He wants to walk and talk with us. God wants His people to know Him.

- What Color is God?

God is Light, Light is all colors.

God is not white, brown, yellow, or black.

God is all colors. We are ALL made like Him.

Why Did God Make People?

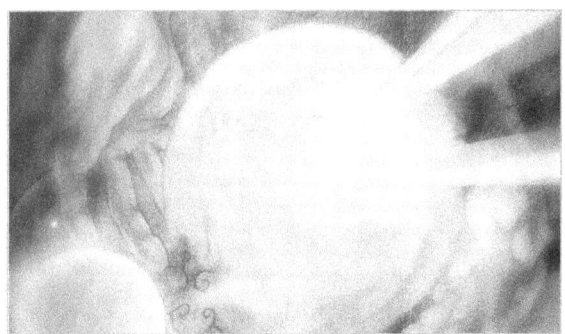

God has everything, can do anything and is so complete in Himself that He does not need anything, so why would He create people?

Since God knows everything, He knew His beautiful people, Adam and Eve, were going to sin. He knew His perfect creation would be damaged by the death and destructiveness which come as direct consequences of living outside of God. So why would He still make people?

God made people because He wanted to have a people who freely chose to know Him, talk with Him and live forever together with Him. God's great Father Heart of Love wanted to share with a people who were His. He knew He would have a people who would love Him and live with Him forever. He knew that if He had a few people who came to know how amazingly beautiful He is they would show others about Him.

> And I will walk among you, and will be your God, and ye shall be my people.
>
> — Leviticus 26:12

> This people have I formed for myself; they shall shew forth my praise.
>
> — Isaiah 43:21

Study the following questions and allow God to reveal to you why He created people.

- How did God make people?

Man was formed by God out of the dust of the earth. He was made in God's image to have dominion over all living things, to have children and to subdue the earth.

> And God said, Let us make man in our image, after our likeness: and let them have dominion over the fish of the sea, and over the fowl of the air, and over the cattle, and over all the earth, and over every creeping thing that creepeth upon the earth. So God created man in his own image, in the image of God created he him; male and female created he them.
>
> — Genesis 1:26

> And the LORD God formed man of the dust of the ground, and breathed into his nostrils the breath of life; and man became a living soul.
>
> — Genesis 2:7

God saw Adam was alone, so He made a woman, Eve, out of a rib he took from Adam's side.

> And the LORD God said, It is not good that the man should be alone; I will make him an help meet for him.
>
> — Genesis 2:18

And the LORD God caused a deep
sleep to fall upon Adam, and he slept:
and he took one of his ribs and
closed up the flesh instead thereof;
22 And the rib, which the LORD God
had taken from man, made he a
woman, and brought her unto
the man.

— Genesis 2:21, 22

- How are we created in God's Image?

When someone says, "You are just like your
Father", they are saying that you talk, walk,
think and act just like your Father, or that
you have special abilities like he does. When
God created us, He gave us special abilities
and characteristics like He has.

We have spiritual abilities to know God,
to talk with Him and to be aware of His
presence.

We have a free will – we can choose. **We
are creative –** we can create.

We have intelligence – we can think, learn,
and understand.

We have authority – we can rule (subdue,
take dominion, organize).

Who is God's One Enemy?

God has one enemy; he is evil and he hates God and hates His people. This enemy will do everything in his wicked power to stop God's plan. This enemy's name is Satan or the Devil.

He came to the Garden of Eden as a serpent, to lie to Adam and Eve. They listened to Satan and sinned. Then they could no longer walk and talk with God. The world became an ugly place, because of sin.

God told them if they disobeyed, **this** would happen.. **This** is called "Death."

Now, men are born with the tendency to sin... It is in their DNA.

People lost the strength to create or choose what is right, and they became slaves to sin and are separated from God.

There's a hard truth that we all have to face sometime: there is God and there is the devil. If you aren't serving God, how are you serving? The Bible calls the devil the father of lies, and having no truth at all!

> He was a murderer from the beginning, not holding to the truth, for there is no truth in him. When he lies, he speaks his native language, for he is a liar and the father of lies.
>
> — John 8:4

God wants each of us to become one His children, and have the same sweet relationship God had with Adam and Eve before they sinned. One way to become His child, is to know who His enemy is and **stay away from him!**

God wants you to become one of His children. God loves you and wants you to know Him and learn His ways. He will save you from the devil's lies and the bondage of sin. **God wants to restore** to you His special characteristics that He gave to Adam. **God wants to bring you back** into "the image of God." You will again be one of His people and **He will be your God.** You will learn to know Him, walk with Him, and talk with Him.

What Is Sin?

Adam and Eve walked and talked to God face to face in the garden.

So what happened? **What was the One Single Don't?**

> And the LORD God commanded the man, saying, Of every tree of the garden thou mayest freely eat: 17 But of the tree of the knowledge of good and evil, thou shalt not eat of it: for in the day that thou eatest thereof thou shalt surely die.
>
> — Genesis 2:16

DO NOT eat of the tree of the knowledge of good and evil.

Rebellion, disobedience, self-will, lying, sneakiness, blame, shame, distrust, suspicion, so many "sins" were stirred up by the only "don't" God gave to Adam and Eve. We really don't need a lot of laws and rules to stir up our sin nature... we really do not like being told what to do and we love to "do our own thing our own way".

Instead of God's way.

> For the wages (payment) of sin is death; but the gift of God is eternal life through Jesus Christ our Lord.
>
> — Romans 6:23

Sin is what drove Adam and Eve out of the garden of Eden.

Ask yourself these questions:

- Is it something that God says is wrong?
- Does it make you sick or unhealthy?
- Do you always have to tell yourself it is right?
- Did you feel guilty/bad when you started doing it?
- Do you have to keep yourself from doing it?
- **Is it sin?**

Sin separates us from God.

God wants to bring us back to Him, so He can walk and talk with us like He did in the Garden of Eden with Adam and Eve.

Let's be honest: it's not always comfortable to admit we've been wrong. We try to find ways to excuse what we do, instead of admitting it's wrong. Maybe you've heard someone say "It's only a *little* lie. It's not that big of a deal!" Maybe you've even said it yourself! But...have you ever thought about how God sees sin? He doesn't care if its big or small. If its sin, its sin!

SIN is ALSO NOT DOING
what we were created to do.

God gives us commands and instructions to follow for our own good. It is to make us into the person He created us to be. It is also to benefit others.

When we do not obey God, it is sin.

What do we do if we SIN?

We must look at sin the way God sees it.

- Run from sin!
- Say yes to God.

- Say no to the devil.
- Get close to God.
- Keep your heart clean.
- Make up your mind: No more!
- Ask God to forgive you from your sin.
- Let God into your life.

Sin isn't just doing the wrong things, but also not doing the things God created you to do. So...what do we do about sin?

Prayer: Lord, I no longer want to do things that keep me from You. Thank for you for showing me ways to walk away from the things that destroy my relationship with You! I choose to love and serve You. Amen.

Look at the list under "What are we supposed to do about sin?" How can you start using this list to turn from sin in your own life?

Who Is Jesus?

> For there is one God and one
> mediator between God and mankind,
> the man Christ Jesus, 6 who gave
> himself as a ransom for all people.
>
> — 1 Timothy 2:5,6

We have all sinned, so now what can we do?
Sin separates from the God who made us.

Sometimes we feel separated and must go
on a journey to find God.

Why are we separated from God?

God, the Creator of the Universe, walked
with Adam and Eve in the garden.

Adam sinned. Adam's sin separated him and
all of his descendants from God.

Adam and Eve became cursed and alone.

Jesus brings us back to God. God sent His only Son, Jesus, to die on the cross for us, is because we are weak to sin.

Jesus is the Son of God.

Jesus is Emmanuel 'God on Earth.'

God sent Jesus to become **"The Ultimate Sacrifice." Jesus became** man to Save man.

Jesus became the sacrifice for our sins. Jesus died for our sins, so we didn't have to die without God.

Jesus not only washes away our sin, but takes from us all past, present, and future sins and works in our hearts that we may not continue to live in sin. When we ask God to forgive us, God gives us power over sin.

Jesus' ultimate sacrifice makes Him our Savior.

After Jesus dies on the cross, **he did not stay dead.** Three days after He was buried, **Jesus rose from the dead**. Jesus is the Messiah; He is the son of God.

> and killed the Prince of life, whom God raised from the dead, of which we are witnesses.

— Acts 3:15

The Resurrection - The Empty Tomb

Now the first *day* of the week Mary Magdalene went to the tomb early, while it was still dark, and saw *that* the stone had been taken away from the tomb. 2 Then she ran and came to Simon Peter, and to the other disciple, whom Jesus loved, and said to them, "They have taken away the Lord out of the tomb, and we do not know where they have laid Him."

3 Peter therefore went out, and the other disciple, and were going to the tomb. 4 So they both ran together, and the other disciple outran Peter and came to the tomb first. 5 And he, stooping down and looking in, saw the linen cloths lying *there;* yet he did not go in. 6 Then Simon Peter came, following him, and went into the tomb; and he saw the linen cloths lying *there,* 7 and the handkerchief that had been around His head, not lying with the linen cloths, but folded together in a place by itself. 8 Then the other disciple, who came to the tomb first, went in also; and he saw and believed.

— John 20: 1-8 NKJV

19 Then, the same day at evening, being the first *day* of the week, when the doors were shut where the disciples were assembled, for fear of the Jews, Jesus came and stood in the midst, and said to them, "Peace *be* with you." 20 When He had said this, He showed them *His* hands and His side. Then the disciples were glad when they saw the Lord.

— John 20:19, 20

We have lots of things that can live in our hearts: dreams, hopes, fears, joy, pain. Some things we don't mind living in our hearts, good memories, our hopes, joy. But there are other things that live in our hearts that we wish we could forget: shame, anger, fear, sadness.

When Jesus lives in our hearts He can change how we think, talk and act. He helps us love those around us, He heals the broken, painful parts in our hearts and minds.

But, He can only live and stay in your heart **if you ask Him.**

What Is Repentance?

We now realize we have a problem. Sin has separated us from God.

How do we get to where God is taking us?

WHAT is the problem?

Because of Adam and Eve's sin, everyone born is separated from God!

WHAT is the Solution?

Repentance!

HUMAN REGRET is not repentance

We cannot just feel guilty when we do something wrong. We must ask for change so we don't continue to sin. We must have godly sorrow.

Feeling guilty is not repentance

Repentance is looking at the sin we have done... God's way. When we do, we become sorry for what we have done, and we don't do it again. **Sometimes, we have to run from sin.**

GODLY SORROW – Godly sorrow leads to doing something about the situation.

Do you have something that you would like to repent from?

Have you asked Jesus the Ultimate Sacrifice to come into your heart and give you a new life?

Or have you found yourself ignoring the sin in your life and doing what you think is right and not looking to what God says is right?

Maybe you would like to pray and ask God for forgiveness, you can pray right now.

What Is Salvation?

Salvation is the gift that comes through accepting Jesus Christ, the "Ultimate Sacrifice," who brings us:

- Back to God,
- Back to who we were created to be
- To Heaven when we die.

When Jesus died on the cross, He took Sin into the grave, He went right into hell, and took the keys that separated us from God, right away from Satan and Jesus won the battle right there for you and I.

That's how Salvation starts and now it's up to us to receive it."

Jesus became the Ultimate Sacrifice. God, the Creator of the Universe, walked with Adam and Eve in the Garden.

Adam sinned. Adam's sin separated him and all of his descendants from God.

Jesus paid the full price for our sins by dying in our place. Now it is up to us to accept Him.

It a process. After we have accepted His Salvation we must allow God guide us in this new life. He has made us a new creature.

> Wherefore, my beloved, as ye have always obeyed, not as in my presence only, but now much more in my absence, work out your own salvation with fear and trembling. 13 For it is God which worketh in you both to will and to do of [his] good pleasure.
>
> — Philippians 2: 12, 13

Jesus is the Ultimate sacrifice.

There is no greater love.

What Must I Do to Be Saved?

that if you confess with your mouth the Lord Jesus and believe in your heart that God has raised Him from the dead, you will be saved.

— Romans 10:9

Jesus wants to give a new heart:

I will give you a new heart and put a new spirit within you. I will take away your heart of stone and give you a heart of flesh. 27 And I will put My Spirit within you and cause you to follow My Laws and be careful to do what I tell you.

— Ezekiel 36:26-27 NLV

Do you want to ask Jesus into your life? Begin by praying a prayer like this from your heart:

Dear Jesus, I know that I have sinned; I have chosen to do things that are wrong when I could have chosen the right way. I repent from those sins; I want and need my life to change... Today.

Please forgive me and place your new heart and your new spirit within me. Please come and live in my heart forever. Jesus, please fill my heart with your love and compassion for others and guide me all of the days of my life. Amen.

How will your life change when Jesus gives you a heart of flesh? If you have prayers this prayer and meant it with all of your heart you have begun the process.

How can we protect this gift?

- Spend time with God and other Believers.
- Walk in the Light, not in sin.
- Find a good church were you can learn God's ways.
- When you make a mistake confess your sins to God, right away.
- Spend time reading your Bible.
- Pray daily.

What Is Water Baptism?

We now realize that we have sinned. And we know that Jesus is the only answer given to us from God to be free from sin.

We have repented from our sins and have asked Jesus into our heart. Jesus has begun the process of removing our heart of stone and giving us a heart of flesh.

The next step is **Water Baptism.**

> "Repent, and let every one of you be baptized in the name of Jesus Christ for the remission of sins; and you shall receive the gift of the Holy Spirit.
>
> — Acts 2:38 NKJV

Water baptism is when a believer is immersed in water, symbolizing the death of Jesus and His resurrection.

What does the word **remission** mean?

Remission means – to **release from the guilt or penalty** of.

For instance, if you owed a large debt and the person said that you no longer had to pay that debt – then you would have a **remission** of debt.

When Jesus died on the cross for you and I he said that we no longer have to pay the debt of sin.

When we are immersed in water baptism it is a **symbol of us dying with Jesus on the cross.**

> Or do you not know that as many of us as were baptized into Christ Jesus were baptized into His death? 4 Therefore we were buried with Him through baptism into death, that just as Christ was raised from the dead by the glory of the Father, even so we also should walk in newness of life.
>
> — Romans 6:3,4 NKJV

When we are raised up out of the water it is a **symbol of Jesus being resurrected.**

When we are water baptized, Jesus says to Satan, "**No longer** will you have control over them. When they go down into that water with Me, **everything** that you have in them is gone."

We come up out of that water with New Life, we come out a new creature, and we come out **sons of God.**

> If we have become one with Christ in His death, we will be one with Him in being raised from the dead to new life. 6 We know that our old life, our old sinful self, was nailed to the cross with Christ. And so the power of sin that held us was destroyed. Sin is no longer our boss.
>
> — Romans 6:5, 6 NLV

We can understand it like this, when we are buried with Jesus by Water Baptism it:

- Destroys the sin nature (the DNA) of Adam.

- Replaces the new nature (the DNA) of Jesus Christ.

For as many of you as were baptized into Christ have put on Christ.

> — Galatians 3:27 NKJV

Therefore, if anyone *is* in Christ, *he is* a new creation; old things have passed away; behold, all things have become new.

> — 2 Corinthians 5:17 NKJV

Through water baptism we are no longer slaves to sin, but we are servants of righteousness.

God has given us the answer.

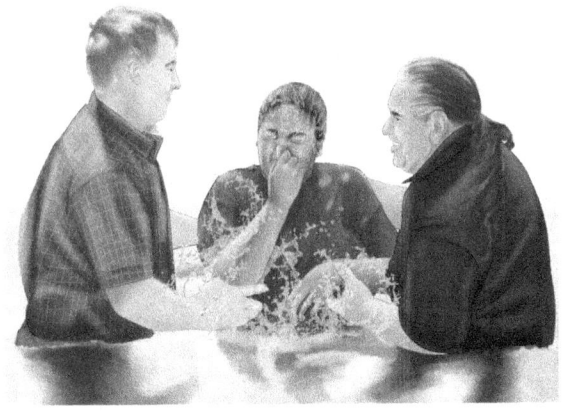

Who is the Holy Spirit?

God is God the Father, Jesus His Son, and the Holy Spirit. That is three persons, but one God. This is called the Trinity.

After Jesus was crucified, he was dead for three days, then God, His Father made Jesus come alive again. Then Jesus went back to heaven to be with His Father. Before Jesus went to heaven, he spent 40 days with his disciples. He promised to send the Holy Spirit to be with them to comfort them, so they would not be alone.

The Holy Spirit teaches people about God. He will comfort you when you feel sad.

Holy Spirit loves to help you when you ask him.

- What is the Baptism of the Holy Spirit?

After Jesus ascended into heaven. Jesus sent the Holy Spirit to His disciples who were together praying, and He baptized them with power and boldness. It was such an amazing experience. They began boldly preaching about Jesus in languages they had never learned and made sick people well.

They were no longer afraid or alone, because the Holy Spirit came to live inside of them, so He was always with them.

Jesus promises this for you too! You can have the baptism of the Holy Spirit, if you ask Him.

It is really important to find a pastor or leader who can teach you the ways of God according to the Bible.

Ask the Holy Spirit to lead you to someone who knows the word of God and will help you.

Go and Make Disciples

Freely you have received, freely give.

A disciple is a follower or student of a teacher.

When Jesus called his disciples, he simply said,

> "Follow me and **I will make you** fishers of men"
>
> — Matthew 4:19 KJV

Jesus taught them to do everything He did, to heal every kind of sickness, cast out devils, and preach about the Kingdom of Heaven.

Just before Jesus went to heaven, He told His disciples to tell the whole world the Good News.

But, How can you follow a God you cannot see?

Follow the Bible. This is our instruction book to teach us what is right. It is God's letter to us.

Follow the Holy Spirit who gives us personal direction since He lives inside of us now. It is natural for you to hear God's voice and be led by the Holy Spirit.

God loves people so much that He sent Jesus to be the Ultimate Sacrifice and die to forgive them of their sins. He wants you to tell people and make disciples of those who will believe your words.

"Go, preach, teach, and baptize and make disciples of all nations."

> Go ye therefore, and teach all nations, baptizing them in the name of the Father, and of the Son, and of the Holy Ghost: 20 Teaching them to observe all things whatsoever I have commanded you: and, lo, I am with you always, [even] unto the end of the world.

> — Matthew 28:19

Acknowledgments

Thank you for granting permission to use the following illustrations:

Pages 2, 4, 5 - Teresa Skinner

Page 4 - Roland Beard from "A Study of Gods Creation"

Page 23 - Larry Cole the "Love" Painting.